What Is a Flood?

ROAD CLOSED

Robin Johnson

 Crabtree Publishing Company
www.crabtreebooks.com

Author: Robin Johnson

Publishing plan research and development: Reagan Miller

Editors: Reagan Miller and Kathy Middleton

Proofreaders: Janine Deschenes

Design and photo research: Samara Parent

Prepress technician: Samara Parent

Print and production coordinator: Kathy Berti

Photographs
iStock: p5; p8; p16; p17 (top), © Philartphace (bottom)
Shutterstock: pp12-13 © ChameleonsEye; p14 © JeremyRichards;
    p15 © Paolo Bona
Wikimedia Commons: p10 © AP Photo/U.S. Coast Guard, Petty
    Officer 2nd Class Kyle Niemi
All other images from Shutterstock

About the author
Robin Johnson has written more than 60 educational books for children. She plans to keep writing books and chasing rainbows—whatever the weather.

Library and Archives Canada Cataloguing in Publication

Johnson, Robin (Robin R.), author
    What is a flood? / Robin Johnson.

(Severe weather close-up)
Includes index.
Issued in print and electronic formats.
ISBN 978-0-7787-2396-7 (bound).--ISBN 978-0-7787-2427-8
(paperback).--ISBN 978-1-4271-1749-6 (html)

    1. Floods--Juvenile literature. I. Title.

GB1399.J65 2016   j551.48'9   C2015-908676-0
                                            C2015-908677-9

Library of Congress Cataloging-in-Publication Data

CIP available at the Library of Congress

Crabtree Publishing Company

Printed in Canada/032016/EF20160210

www.crabtreebooks.com   1-800-387-7650

Published in Canada
Crabtree Publishing
616 Welland Ave.
St. Catharines, Ontario
L2M 5V6

Published in the United States
Crabtree Publishing
PMB 59051
350 Fifth Avenue, 59th Floor
New York, New York 10118

Published in the United Kingdom
Crabtree Publishing
Maritime House
Basin Road North, Hove
BN41 1WR

Published in Australia
Crabtree Publishing
3 Charles Street
Coburg North
VIC 3058

Contents

Changing weather

Have you ever been caught in the rain? The **weather** can change very fast! Weather is what the air and sky are like in a certain place at a certain time. On a hot, sunny day, you'll want to cool off in a wading pool. Then suddenly it begins to rain! You hope the rain will go away and come again another day.

What do you
ThinK?

What would happen if a lot of rain fell in your wading pool all at once?

Rainy weather

Sometimes rain falls lightly. You can reach out your hand and feel the soft, cool drops. But sometimes when it rains, it pours! You run inside before you get soaked. You listen to the rain pound on your roof. You watch huge puddles grow. Soon the water will be gone again.

Moving water

Water is always moving around Earth. Rain, snow, and other types of **precipitation** fall from the clouds. Some of the water soaks into the ground. Some of the water falls into rivers, lakes, oceans—and kiddie pools!

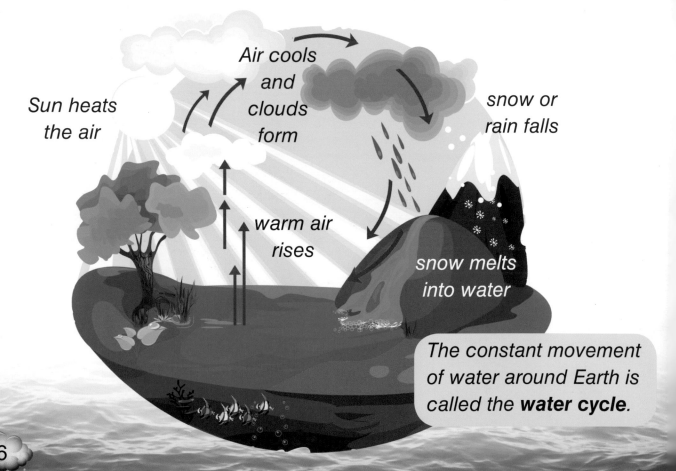

Sun heats the air

Air cools and clouds form

snow or rain falls

warm air rises

snow melts into water

The constant movement of water around Earth is called the **water cycle**.

Up, up, and away

Heat from the Sun causes warm air to rise and water to **evaporate**. To evaporate means to change from water into **water vapor**, or a thin mist of water in the air. As the warm air rises, it brings water vapor high into the sky. When the air cools, the water vapor in the air also cools and forms clouds. Then, rain and snow fall from the clouds, and the cycle starts again.

People, animals, and plants need water to live.

Severe weather

The water cycle moves water all around the world. Different places get different amounts of water at different times. **Severe weather** can bring huge amounts of water to an area in the form of rain or snow. Severe weather is weather that can hurt people and animals, and cause damage to land or buildings. **Hurricanes** and **blizzards** are examples of severe weather.

A hurricane is a huge **storm** with heavy rain. Hurricanes start over ocean waters. They have very strong **winds**, or moving air, that can push water onto land.

Floods

Severe weather can cause **floods**. A flood happens when water flows onto land that is normally dry. It is a type of **natural disaster**. Floods can destroy trees and **crops**. Crops are plants grown by farmers for food. Floods can fill cars and homes with water. Very powerful floods can wash away roads, bridges, and buildings!

The water in a flood may be just a few inches or centimeters deep. Sometimes, it can be as high as a house!

What causes floods?

Most of the city of New Orleans, Louisiana, was flooded by a powerful hurricane in 2005. Strong winds and rushing water caused a lot of damage.

Floods happen for many reasons. If a lot of rain falls in a short amount of time, rivers can **overflow**, or spill over their sides. Storms with high winds can wash ocean waves onto areas of land that are usually dry, such as roads. Floods can also happen if a lot of snow **melts** faster than the ground can soak it up. When snow melts, it turns into liquid water that flows.

Levees and dams

People build **levees** and **dams** to control water. Levees are walls built along the sides of a river. They stop the river from flooding towns and cities. A dam is a structure across a river that controls the flow of its water. If levees or dams break, huge amounts of water suddenly flood onto dry land. Levees and dams can be damaged by ships, fallen trees, or large objects. Rushing water can also wear them away over time.

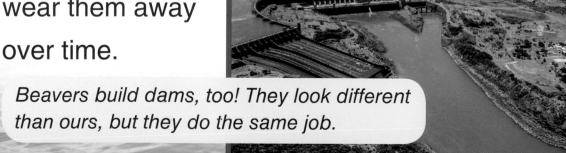

beaver dam

dam

Beavers build dams, too! They look different than ours, but they do the same job.

Rising waters

Most floods happen slowly. The water in an area rises over a period of days or weeks. People usually have some time to get ready for the floods or go somewhere safe. Some floods happen very fast, however. People must hurry to safety before the water rushes in.

Flash floods are powerful floods that happen quickly with very little warning.

Flash floods

Flash floods are the fastest and most dangerous floods. They can cover an area with water in just a few hours—or even minutes! Flash floods happen when dams or levees break. They also occur when sudden, heavy rain falls into rivers. Water pours over the sides of the rivers and rushes onto land.

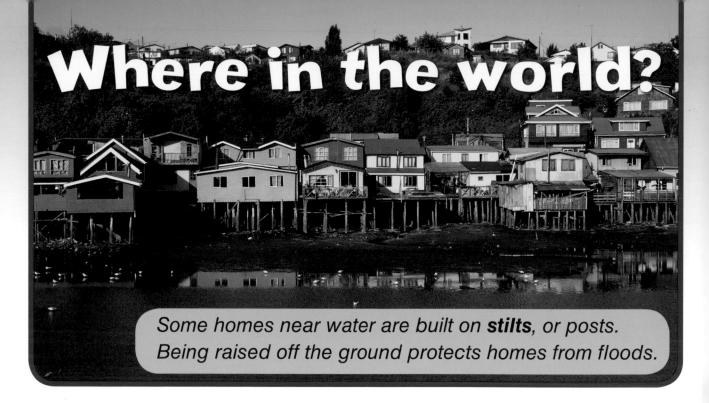

Where in the world?

*Some homes near water are built on **stilts**, or posts. Being raised off the ground protects homes from floods.*

Floods can happen anywhere where rain falls. Flooding is more likely to occur in some areas than others, however. Places near water have more floods than places far from water because rivers, lakes, and oceans sometimes overflow. Places down in **valleys** are also more likely to have floods than places high up on hills because water flows from higher ground to lower ground.

When do floods happen?

Floods can happen any time of the year. Warm areas of the world have a **rainy season**. That is the time of year when these places get the most rain and flooding. In snowy areas, floods can happen when the weather warms up. Sudden high **temperatures** can cause snow to melt faster than the ground can soak it up.

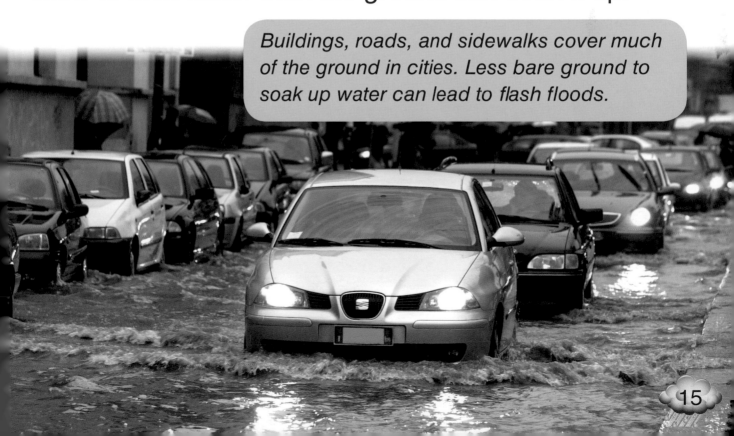

Buildings, roads, and sidewalks cover much of the ground in cities. Less bare ground to soak up water can lead to flash floods.

Water watchers

Meteorologists watch the weather and warn us if floods may occur. Meteorologists are scientists who study weather. They measure how much precipitation falls in an area. They track severe weather that could cause floods. Then they try to **predict** where and when floods will occur. To predict is to tell what will happen before it takes place.

Watches and warnings

Meteorologists warn us about possible flooding, so we can get ready for them or go somewhere safe. They give their reports on television, on the radio, and online. A **flood watch** means that a flood could possibly happen in your area. A **flood warning** means that a flood is about to happen or is already taking place near you.

People stack bags of sand to build levees to stop rivers from overflowing.

Make a plan

If your home is in an area at risk for floods, your family should make a **disaster plan**. This is a list of the steps your family will follow if there is a flood or other natural disaster. You should decide where to meet if your home is not safe. How will you get there? What will you bring?

This family is planning for a rainy day! They are making a disaster plan in case there is a flood near their home.

EMERGENCY PREPARATION CHECKLIST

Section 1: Emergency Survival Items:

- ☐ Water Containers
- ☐ First Aid Kit
- ☐ Flashlight
- ☐ Battery Operated Radio
- ☐ Batteries
- ☐ Food

Make a kit

Help your family gather items for a disaster kit. The kit should contain all the supplies you would need to survive for a few days. Some of the items you might put in your kit are: first aid kit, bottled water, canned food, can opener, a radio that runs on batteries, flashlights, extra batteries, and blankets.

What do you Think?

What are some other plans you should make with your family in case of a flood?

ROAD FLOODED

During a flood, hurry to a safe place away from rising water. Go to the highest floor of your house or other strong building. You and your family may be told by police to **evacuate** your home for a while if it is not safe to stay there. Never walk or drive through water to get to safety, however. Flood waters can be very powerful. It only takes six inches (15 centimeters) of rushing water to knock down an adult!

A car can be carried away by as little as two feet (60 centimeters) of flowing water!

After a flood

After a flood is over, there may still be water in your home or yard. The water is not clean and could make you sick. Do not swim or walk in the water, or play with any toys that have gotten wet. Avoid drinking tap water until an adult tells you it is clean. Stay out of buildings that were damaged in the flood. They may look safe, but water can weaken the base of buildings. This could make the building fall.

What do you Think?

What might people need after a flood if buildings and crops were damaged?

21

Make a model

Build a **model** to see how a flood works!

Follow these steps:

1. Fill a container with water.

2. Use modeling clay to form the bottom of a river down the middle of the container. Build up small mounds on each side to form its banks

3. Fill the rest of the container outside the river with soil.

4. Add trees, houses, or other things to your model along the river's banks.

5. Slowly pour water into your river.

What happens when there is too much water in the river?

water

container

modeling clay

toy tree and house

soil

What do you Think?

How could you help protect the houses in your model from a flood?

Learning more

Books

The Water Cycle by Bobbie Kalman and Rebecca Sjonger. Crabtree Publishing Company, 2006.

Floods by Libby Koponen. Scholastic, 2009.

What is precipitation? by Robin Johnson. Crabtree Publishing Company, 2013.

Floods: Be Aware and Prepare by Renée Gray-Wilburn. Capstone Press, 2014.

Websites

This useful website tells you what to do before, during, and after floods:

www.ready.gov/kids/know-the-facts/floods

Visit this website for fascinating facts and tips on floods:

http://eschooltoday.com/natural-disasters/floods/what-is-a-flood.html

Be a weather whiz kid and learn all about rain and floods at this website:

www.weatherwizkids.com/weather-rain.htm

Learn about floods, precipitation, temperature, and more at this website:

http://extension.illinois.edu/treehouse/rockweather.cfm?Slide=16

Search for dangers floating in flood waters in this online game:

www.vicses.com.au/floodsafe-game/

Words to know

Note: Some boldfaced words are defined where they appear in the book.

blizzard (BLIZ-erd) noun A storm with heavy snowfall and strong winds

evacuate (ih-VAK-yoo-eyt) verb To leave a place of danger

flood (fluhd) noun Water flowing onto land that is normally dry

melt (melt) verb To change from solid to liquid form by heating

model (MOD-l) noun A representation of a real object

natural disaster (NACH-er-uhl dih-ZAS-ter) adjective, noun An event in nature that harms people and causes a lot of damage

overflow (oh-ver-FLOH) verb To spill over the top or side of something

precipitation (pri-sip-i-TEY-shuhn) noun Rain, snow, or other water that falls from clouds

storm (stawrm) noun A period of very bad weather

temperature (TEHM-per-a-chur) noun A measure of how hot or cold something is

valley (VAL-ee) noun An area of low land between hills

> A *noun* is a person, place, or thing. A *verb* is an action word that tells you what someone or something does. An *adjective* is a word that tells you what something is like.

Index